The Concert

Thelma Page

Illustrated by Jacqui Thomas

OXFORD

UNIVERSITY PRESS

OXFORD

UNIVERSITY PRESS

Great Clarendon Street, Oxford OX2 6DP

Oxford University Press is a department of the University of Oxford.
It furthers the University's objective of excellence in research, scholarship,
and education by publishing worldwide in

Oxford New York

Auckland Bangkok Buenos Aires Cape Town Chennai
Dar es Salaam Delhi Hong Kong Istanbul Karachi Kolkata
Kuala Lumpur Madrid Melbourne Mexico City Mumbai Nairobi
São Paulo Shanghai Singapore Taipei Tokyo Toronto

Oxford is a registered trade mark of Oxford University Press
in the UK and in certain other countries

British Library Cataloguing in Publication Data

Data available

ISBN 0 19 919506 4

1 3 5 7 9 10 8 6 4 2

Printed in Hong Kong

<h1 style="text-align:center">1</h1>

May-Ling liked school. She had only been at
Swan Lane for a few weeks but she had been
happy from the first day. It was lucky that
Robert was in the same class. Robert lived
next door to May-Ling. When they could,
they worked together in class.

One morning Mrs Kumar read the story of 'Toad of Toad Hall'. Toad was a noisy character. He liked showing off to the animals who lived in the woods and along the riverbank.

The story reminded Robert of a joke and he whispered it to May-Ling. So he missed what Mrs Kumar said next.

'We are going to act the story of "Toad of
Toad Hall" at the end of term concert,' said
Mrs Kumar. 'We will invite your parents to
come and watch, so we must do it really well.'

Rachel put her hand up. 'Can I be Toad in
the play?'

'Don't be silly,' interrupted Michael. 'Toad is
a boy. You can tell from the story. I could do it.
It would be great driving the car!'

'We can have a boy or a girl,' answered Mrs
Kumar. 'We just need to find the best person.'
'The best person for what?' asked Robert,
starting to listen again.
'I have just been explaining that we are
going to act the story of "Toad of Toad Hall".
The part of Toad can be a boy or a girl,'
Mrs Kumar repeated patiently. 'Please try to
listen, Robert.

'Now it's playtime. Anyone who would like
to be Toad can stay here and try reading the
words. I need to choose someone with a good
memory and a clear speaking voice. Everyone
else can go out to play.'

2

At playtime about half the class stayed in to
read for the part. 'I want to drive around in
Toad's fast car,' said Michael, showing how
he would turn the steering wheel and hoot
the hooter.

'I go to acting class on Saturdays,' said
Rachel, 'so I know what to do. I hope
Mrs Kumar chooses me.'

Mrs Kumar asked everyone in turn to read some of Toad's words. Tom read well but he was much too quiet. Michael was so excited that he read much too fast. May-Ling read very carefully but she was a bit shy. Rachel sounded as if she were Toad already. Her voice was clear and confident. Robert was nearly as good.

'Remember, there are lots of other animals, so don't be upset if you are not chosen,' said Mrs Kumar. 'Everyone will do something. We don't have much time, so the person I choose for Toad will have to be someone who doesn't need a lot of practice. Thank you all for staying in. Now go and play and I'll tell you later who will be Toad.'

In the playground, May-Ling went off with
Robert to talk about it.

'I think you were the best,' said May-Ling.
'I hope she chooses you.'

'I think she should choose me,' interrupted
Rachel. 'I know I could be really good as Toad.'

Robert knew Rachel had read the part well, but Toad was a funny character and it would be fun to act the part. Robert liked making people laugh and it would be exciting to have a big audience. He hoped Mrs Kumar would choose him.

12

At home time Mrs Kumar had lots of papers
to hand out.

'I'd like you to practise your words for the
play at home,' she explained. 'Even if you only
have a few words to say, stand at the top of the
stairs and say the words loudly to someone at
the bottom.'

'What if you don't have any stairs?' called out Michael.

'I'm sure you'll think of something,' replied Mrs Kumar.

'Rachel and Robert, I'd like both of you to learn the words for Toad.'

Robert looked pleased. He took the papers and started reading to himself.

'But who will be Toad in the play?' asked
Rachel. 'I don't want to learn all those words
and then not do it.'

'Well, we've decided to do the play twice,'
explained Mrs Kumar. 'The hall isn't very
big and it means it won't be such a squash
for the audience if we do it on two days.
So you and Robert will each have a turn.'

Everyone took their words and rushed
off home.

3

The next week they practised part of the play every day. There were songs to learn, recorder music to practise, and dances to fit in. They made animal masks and painted them. They painted huge trees for scenery.

Then they made the car for Toad. It was the side view of a car cut out of a large piece of cardboard and painted. If Toad held it in the right place his head would be seen through the window.

When they practised the play Rachel and
Robert took turns to read Toad's part. Robert
kept leaving his words at home. He said that he
knew them, but he got stuck, and Mrs Kumar
had to remind him what to say.

Everyone had to remember when it was their
turn to say their words, sing, or dance, or play
the recorder. It all seemed an enormous muddle,
not like a play at all.

'The next time we practise, I would like you to say your words, not read them,' Mrs Kumar told them. 'Please practise at home. We only have a week left to get everything right. Don't forget to bring your clothes for the play on Monday so that we can have a dress rehearsal.'

'I'm never going to learn it all,' whispered
Robert to May-Ling when they were back in
the classroom. 'I just can't remember what
comes next. I didn't realize there would be
so much to learn.'

'You'll be fine. You just need a bit more
practice,' answered May-Ling. 'Come round
to my house tonight and I'll help you.'

Rachel overheard.

'Can I come too, please? I really need to practise. My mum never has time to help me. Please, can I?'

'I'll ask my mum,' replied May-Ling.

May-Ling knew that Rachel could be a bit bossy so she hoped her mum would say no. But she said, 'Yes, of course Rachel can come, as long as she asks her mum.'

All three walked home together.

'I'm looking forward to the dress rehearsal,'
said May-Ling. 'It will be much better when
we all have costumes.'

'My mum has got some special face paint
and I'm going to have a green face and green
hands,' said Rachel. 'I'll ask her to do the
same for you, Robert, if you like.'

'OK, thanks,' said Robert.

They went indoors and May-Ling's mum gave
them a drink. Then they went to May-Ling's
room to practise. It was just as May-Ling had
thought. Rachel told Robert where to sit and
what to do. They took turns to read.

They giggled at the funny bits and helped
each other.

Robert made jokes and they laughed even
more. At first it was fun just to listen, but
then May-Ling got bored.

22

'Shall I read the words for the other animals?' suggested May-Ling.

'No, it's OK, thanks,' said Rachel, 'It's easier if we take turns to read the bits in between. Go on, Robert, you read the next bit.'

There was nothing for May-Ling to do.
She felt left out.

Now Robert was Rachel's friend.

She wished Rachel hadn't come. It would
have been much better without her.

Rachel and Robert didn't notice when
May-Ling went downstairs.

She switched on the television.

She could hear laughing from the other two
as Robert read the words in funny voices.

May-Ling was glad when her mum said tea
was ready. She called to the other two to come
down. Now perhaps they would forget about the
play for a while.

But all through tea Robert and Rachel were
saying their words and getting them wrong on
purpose to make each other laugh.

Then May-Ling had an idea.

After tea she said, 'Give me your words.
I'm going to test you both. It's time to practise
properly. By the time you go home you will
know these words.'

She made them stand at the top of the stairs and she stood at the bottom.

Then she called out their names. They had to remember what came next. May-Ling helped them when they forgot and called out, 'I can't hear you,' when they mumbled.

When May-Ling's mum said it was time for
them to go home, May-Ling begged for ten
minutes more, so that they could get to the end.
They had been through the whole play twice.
The second time Rachel and Robert hadn't
needed much help.

As Rachel was leaving she said, 'Thanks,
May-Ling, we both know the words now.'
'Yes, I'm not worried any more,' added
Robert. 'I know I can do it. Thanks, May-Ling.'

4

Rachel's parents and her grandad came to
see her in the play on Wednesday. Robert's
mum and dad came to see him on Thursday.
Everyone knew their words and the recorders
played the right notes. The dancers remembered
their dances. The audience laughed at the
funny bits.

At the end the clapping went on and on.
Mrs Kumar said thank-you to everyone who
had helped to make the play a success.

Robert and Rachel looked at May-Ling and
joined in the clapping. May-Ling was really
happy. She knew that Robert and Rachel were
both her special friends.